Oodles of

HORSES

**A collection of
posters, doodles, cards, stencils, crafts,
stickers, frames—and lots more—for girls
who love horses!**

★ American Girl®

Published by American Girl Publishing. Copyright © 2010 American Girl

Questions or comments? Call 1-800-845-0005, visit **americangirl.com**, or write to Customer Service, American Girl, 8400 Fairway Place, Middleton, WI 53562-0497.

Printed in China
13 14 15 16 17 18 LEO 10 9 8 7 6 5 4

Editorial Development: Trula Magruder

Art Direction & Design: Camela Decaire

Production: Jeannette Bailey, Sarah Boecher, Meagan Eggers, Tami Kepler, Judith Lary

Illustrations: Nila Aye, Helen Dardik, Janell Genovese, Lori Joy Smith, Shawn Banner

Tabletop Photography: Radlund Photography, Mike Walker, Chris Hynes, Jim Jordan

Photography: p. 7, four horses—© iStockphoto/Ivenks; p. 8, laughing horse—© iStockphoto/Travis Pacheco; p. 49, horseshoe—© iStockphoto/futureimage; p. 65, horses along fence—© iStockphoto/lillisphotography; p. 66, pony in field—© iStockphoto/orava; p. 68, pony points—© Gemma Giannini/Grant Heilman Photography, Inc.

Craft Stylists: Carrie Anton, Jessica Hastreiter

Dear Reader,

You don't need to ride in rodeos, star in show jumping, or parade in pony pageants to enjoy this book. You don't even need to own a horse to have fun trotting—or galloping—through these pages. But to get the most from these activities, you do need to love horses!

We've packed these pages with projects that let horses shine, from horse photos and pony puzzles to equine quizzes and cowgirl crafts.

So saddle up for a fun-filled exploration of the horse—without even leaving your bedroom.

Your friends at American Girl

Horse Sense

Are you an equine expert? Take this quiz to find out! Circle your answers, and then check them on the next page.

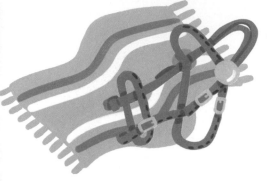

1. Bridles, bits, blankets, and brushes are some of the items in a horse's

   a. tick.
   b. tack.
   c. tock.
   d. toe.

2. Which sport does NOT require a horse?

   a. polo
   b. dressage
   c. barrel racing
   d. luge

3. Which object is NOT part of a saddle?

   a. drum
   b. horn
   c. seat
   d. pommel

4. Which of these horses can actually pull a plow?

   a. unicorn
   b. pommel horse
   c. draft horse
   d. hobby horse

5. A cinch is a strap used to hold on a

- **a.** bridle.
- **c.** saddle.
- **b.** horse blanket.
- **d.** cart.

6. True or false: Some horses have feathers.

- **a.** true
- **b.** false

7. Which one of these surfaces is slippery for horses wearing horseshoes?

- **a.** pavement
- **c.** grass
- **b.** dirt
- **d.** rocks

8. Which feeding rule is false?

- **a.** Feed treats from buckets.
- **b.** Keep hay and grasses available so that horses get enough food and don't get bored.
- **c.** Horses don't care when they get fed, as long as they get fed.
- **d.** Keep a fence between you and the horse when feeding it.

Answers

1. b; 2. d—In luge, athletes ride a sled feet-first down a track; 3. a; 4. c—Draft horses are known as "quiet giants" because they have patience and strength; 5. c; 6. a— Horses have long feathered hairs that hang down over their hooves; 7. a; 8. c.

Yee-ha-ha!

Share these horselaughs with friends. For more giggles, hang up the poster at right.

What's as big as a horse but doesn't weigh anything?

a horse's shadow

What has two heads, four eyes, six legs, and a tail?

a horse and her rider

What's a horse's favorite game?

stable tennis

What does it mean if you find a horseshoe?

Some horse is walking around in her socks.

Where do veterinarians send sick horses?

to the horse-pital

Horses always root for what sports team?

the Colts

give her one of yours.

Pony Express

Fill out these *neigh*borly notes, fold them, and pass them to pals.

Yippee!

I can't wait to tell you
what just happened.

_____

_____

_____

Whoa!

I need to tell you
a secret.

_____

_____

_____

Hey, Pardner

I need someone to
really listen.

_____

_____

_____

Giddyup!

Grab your gear and
meet me at

_____

_____

_____

From:

To:

From:

To:

From:

To:

From:

To:

The Mane Event

Mark your calendar for this fun time:

....

....

Yea or Neigh?

Circle your choice.
Can you come
over tonight?

Yes!

I can't.

I need to ask first.

Pass it back!

Ready to Hoof It . . .

○ to recess?
○ to the park?
○ to my room?
○ to my backyard?

Let's Ride Together . . .

○ to school.
○ to practice.
○ to town.
○ to the movies.

From:

To:

From:

To:

From:

To:

From:

To:

Nicker Names

Try these ideas for naming horses. To practice, name your plush ponies, your plastic pintos—or your real horses!

My Horse

Choose a spice.

- Pepper
- Cinnamon
- Cayenne

Choose
a word that means "speedy" *and* a name that matches the first letter of that word.

- Bettie Bolt
- Rapid Rita
- Billy Blaze

Choose a bug.

- Ladybug
- Firefly
- Katydid

Choose
a Western name *and* a weather-related word.

- Cheyenne Storm
- Wyatt Lightning
- Tornado Tex

Choose a food you love.

- Pancake
- Strawberry
- Cookie

Choose
a three-letter name *and* something you'd find in the desert.

- Tom Sands
- Lil Cactus
- Sam Snake

Choose a jewel.

- Diamond
- Ruby
- Sapphire

Choose
a state name *and* a pretty-sounding name.

- Colorado Dreamer
- Dakota Magic
- Montana Mist

Choose a reindeer name.

- Dasher
- Dancer
- Cupid

Rodeo Room

To give your room cowgirl spirit, add plastic horses!

Reflect on your favorite horses!
Attach plastic horses to the
border of a mirror with jewel glue.
Let dry.

Tame messages with horse magnets. Cut small strips from a roll of adhesive magnetic tape. Attach the strips to the backs of small plastic horses. Stick the magnets to a metal surface.

Hitch your favorite horse photo to a frame. Write fun phrases with letter stickers, and glue on rhinestones and plastic horses.

Pony Practice

Horse around with this head until you can draw it without the directions.

Start with a 4 like this.

Attach an M

with a long tail.

Draw a face and a mane.

Built 4 speed!

Tall Tails

Rein in your reading with these bookmarks.

Get a kick out of books!

SADDLE UP

for some

tall tails

&

mane

events!

Reading Round up Reading Round up Reading Round up Reading Round up

Add a horse's tail to your bookmark. Punch a hole on the top edge and tie on a few strands of yarn.

SADDLE
UP

for some
tail tails
&
mane
events!

★ AmericanGirl.

Slip a bookmark between the pages of a horse book and give it to a horse fan!

Pony Papers

Brand your horse scrapbooks or crafts with these pretty papers.

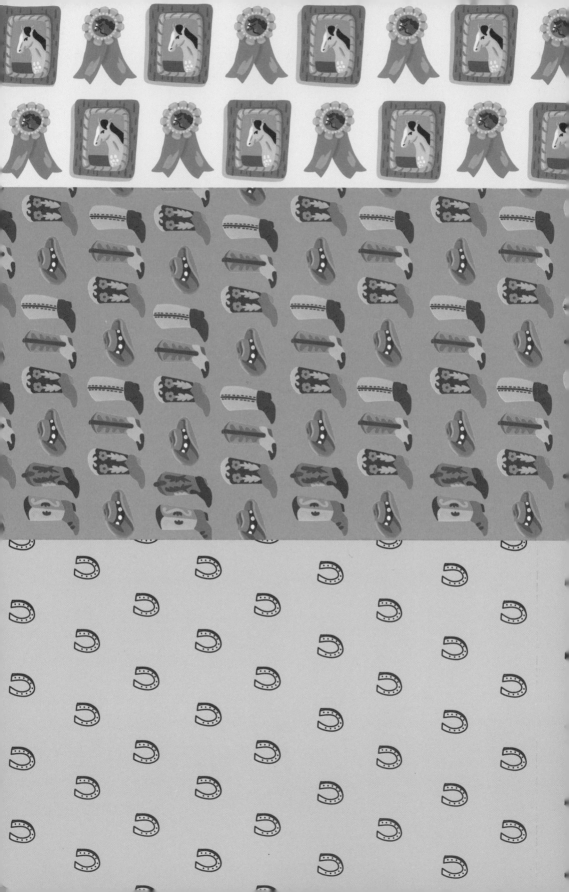

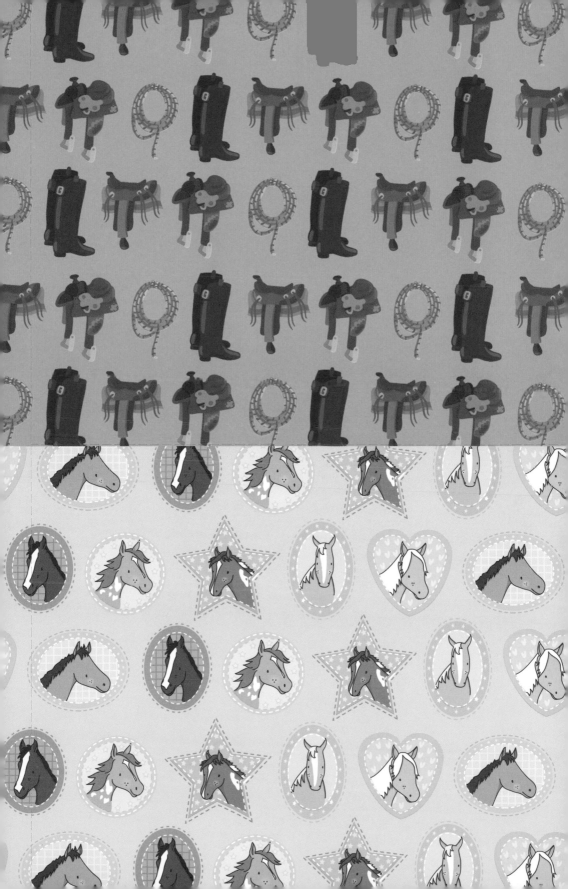

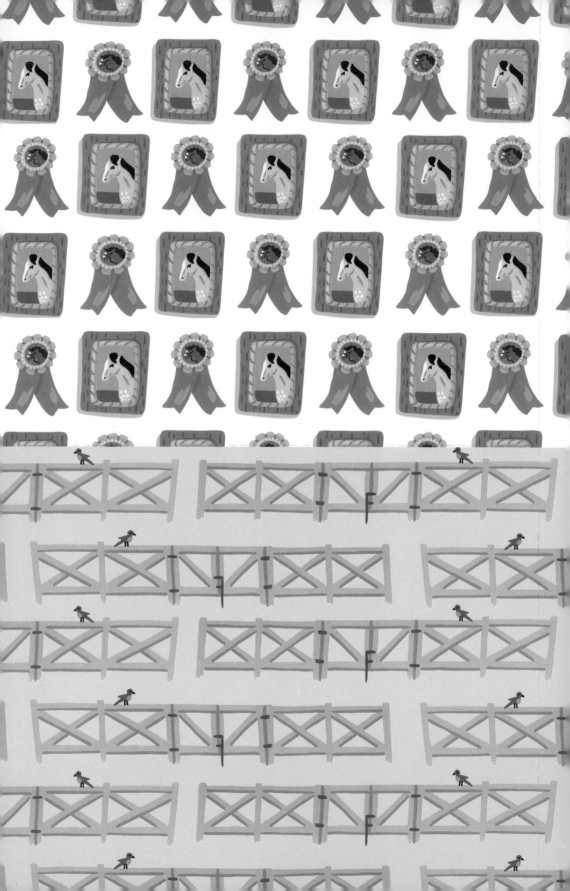

Saddle Sayings

Circle the correct meaning of these fun horse phrases.

1. I wish my brother would **get off his high horse.**

   a. climb off a horse bred for tall boys

   b. stop acting more important than others

   c. quit acting upset

2. Our teacher was **champing at the bit** to hand out tests.

   a. angry

   b. too tired

   c. impatient

3. Alice needs to **pony up** for the pizza party.

   a. ride to a designated area

   b. pay what she owes

   c. try something new

4. My dad **has a lot of horse sense.**

   a. knows a lot about horses

   b. has a good sense of smell

   c. has common sense

5. I got the information **straight from the horse's mouth.**

   a. straight from the source

   b. straight from a talking horse

   c. straight from a horse trainer

6. My sister **eats like a horse** when we have tacos.

   a. nibbles on her food

   b. makes a mess when she eats

   c. eats a lot of food

7. Emma always **puts the cart before the horse!**

   a. offers a bargain

   b. does things out of order

   c. shares with everyone

8. My friend moved to a **one-horse town.**

   a. a small town

   b. a big city without horses

   c. a town where everyone has a horse

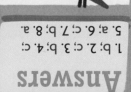

Horse Show

Display, accessorize, or play with these paper horses.

Punch out these horses and their stands. Fold the stands in half, and slide the base of each horse into the slots on each stand. Use the longer stands for the horses with wider bases.

- To corral your horses together, fold paper for fences. You can also use the fences to create a show-jumping arena.

- Draw and cut out blue ribbons for show winners.

- Fold paper over the horses' backs for blankets.

Cowgirl Chic

Display your passion for ponies with a horse-lover's headband.

1. To start, create a 3-D paper flower. To make one, layer 3 flat paper flowers on top of one another, using Glue Dots between the layers. (Look for paper flowers at craft and scrapbook stores.)

2. Press a horse sticker onto the center of the flower. Attach the flower to a plastic headband with craft glue. Let dry.

Fortune Teller

Will you have horses in your future? Find out!

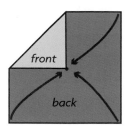 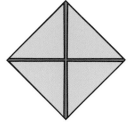 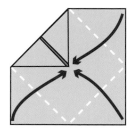 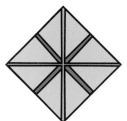

1. Fold each corner point into the center of the back side (marked with a dot).

2. Flip so that the flaps are facedown. Fold each corner into the center.

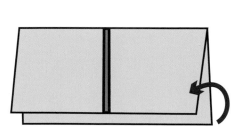

3. Fold in half to crease.

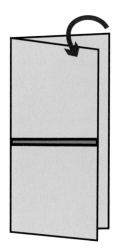

4. Unfold, and fold in half the other way.

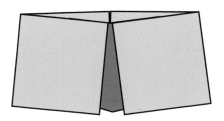

5. Stick your thumbs and first two fingers into the four pockets. Push all the pockets to the center to begin playing.

TO USE:

1. Choose a word on top of the fortune teller.

2. Open and close the center points the same number of times as the number of letters in the word, alternating sides.

3. Pick a number. Open and close the center points as many times as the number.

4. Pick another number. Open the flap, and read your fortune.

canter

trot

You'll be the voice of an animated horse on TV.

You'll travel the world buying show ponies.

You'll become a riding instructor.

You'll become a famous horse trainer.

You'll write a best-selling novel about a wild horse.

You'll become a judge for horse shows.

gallop

run

You'll own a ranch and raise quarter horses.

You'll become a vet who specializes in horses.

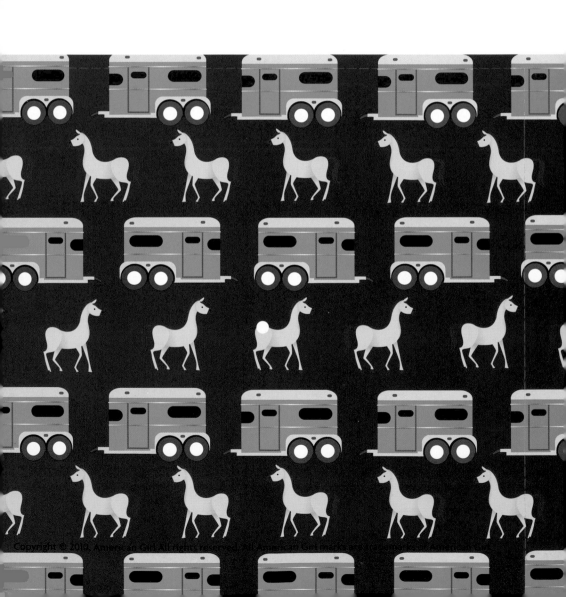

Horse Laughs

Invite friends over to horse around with this game.

For this fortune teller, instead of choosing a fortune, you'll choose a silly action to perform. Round up a group of friends to play. For even more laughs, ask each player to continue her action until everyone is acting out one. Then play again!

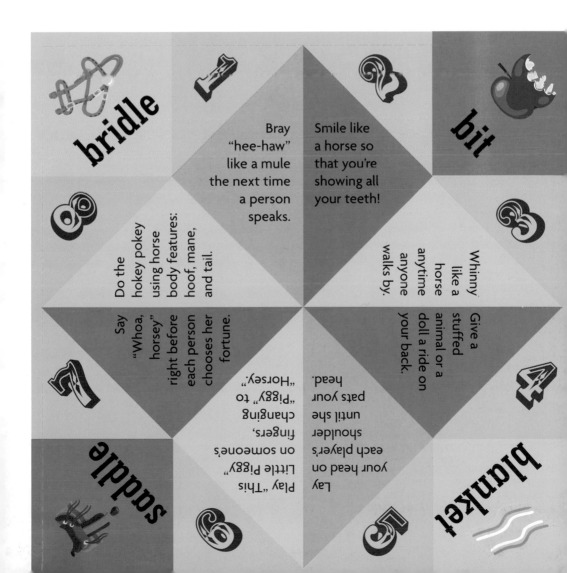

bridle

bit

saddle

blanket

Bray "hee-haw" like a mule the next time a person speaks.

Smile like a horse so that you're showing all your teeth!

Do the hokey pokey using horse body features: hoof, mane, and tail.

Whinny like a stuffed horse animal or a anytime doll a ride on anyone your back. walks by. Give a

Say "Whoa, horsey" right before each person chooses her fortune.

Play "This Little Piggy" on someone's fingers, changing "Piggy" to "Horsey."

Lay your head on each player's shoulder until she pats your head.

Pony Practice

Doodle this head again and again. Then, after you've practiced, draw the picture for your art collection.

Start with two lines running downhill.

Make this shape.

Add a face,

Perky ears, and a broad neck.

Drawing beautiful hair is the mane event.

Stable Stencils

Create cowgirl arts and crafts with horse stencils.

Pull out the stencil at right. Lay the stencil on paper or fabric, and draw around the inside of the horse shape. Remove the stencil to color or cut out the horse.

Ideas for using stencils:

- Design horse posters for school projects, your locker, or your room.

- Create horse art for scrapbook pages.

- Draw dozens of overlapping horses for a cowgirl collage.

- Cut out a fabric horse, and attach it to the front of a tee with fabric glue. Let dry.

Ask an adult for permission before you permanently glue down any horses.

Cowgirl Coupons

Share these caring coupons with your sidekicks.

Horse
Race

This coupon is good for a full recess of running around!

Mane
Event

Turn in this coupon, and I'll style your hair for a special event or just for fun.

Lasso Me In

Want a friendly face at your next game or competition? Redeem this coupon, and I'll ride along.

Here's a
Leg Up

Need help cleaning, studying, or practicing? This coupon is good for an all-day helper.

Horse
Show

Present this coupon and you can pick the movie—with no arguments from me.

From the
Chuck Wagon

This coupon entitles you to a treat prepared by me!

To create more coupons, make a double-sided copy of this page.

Option: Bundle up *all* of these coupons and give them to a favorite person.

To:

From:

To:

From:

To:

From:

To:

From:

To:

From:

To:

From:

Filly Frames

Display your friends' photos inside these mini frames.

Fortunate Foot

Try your luck with your very own horseshoe!

People in many cultures believe that horseshoes

BRING GOOD LUCK.

The trick, though, is deciding which way to hang your shoe!

• Some people believe that the ends should point up to keep your luck collected in the "cup."

• Others think the ends should point down so that the luck flows onto you as you walk underneath the horseshoe.

 Ask an adult to help you tape or tack this horseshoe over a doorway in your room.

Pony Post

Send these precious postcards to faraway friends.

To:

To:

Horse Tracks

Is that graffiti on the barn or a message for horse fans? Start at the top and read the lines from left to right. Underline any words two letters or longer that you find. What's the message?

E F K L K T H E X R S C X A R T G
C O F R I J I K M F Y O T E J I X
D F W F R I D I N G C B I O W U F
H U Y R H U V G A K T W I S C H V
B R K E E P I N G W S Y O M F O T
A E T H E O V H K N C R I X U Y O
E F Y U N R J L H O R S E C F U D
T B E T W E E N Y E G I K Y J E R
B F P L K N Y O U U C B H Y W P P
H I R R H U W X O W T J A N D H K
T I T H E O D Y I W S Y E H F E T
D E T K N I C G E G R O U N D R P

Wild Cards

Want to wow your friends? Tell them these fun horse facts.

All racing thoroughbreds born in the United States, Canada, and Europe celebrate their birthdays on exactly the same day—January 1! It's an easier way to track the horses' ages for horse racing. Gee, all the other horses must get lots of party invitations on that day!

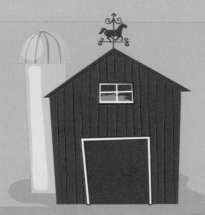

Horses need only two to three hours' sleep a day—and they get most of that standing up. A horse locks a joint in her back leg, and that joint signals the muscles to relax but not collapse. Now the horse can snooze. Too bad humans can't do that while waiting in long lines!

Open your mouth and take a breath. Horses can't do that. They can breathe only through their noses. Flaps at the back of a horse's throat work like trap-doors, allowing only food and water into the stomach and air into the lungs. Having a stuffy nose must be a lot more stressful when you're a horse.

Horses like to stand head to tail and side by side. Why? A horse might answer, "You swish the flies from my face and I'll swish the flies from yours!"

Name: Welsh Pony
Color: Any solid
Characteristics:
Athletic and intelligent;
a popular show pony

© Kit Houghton
Photography/Corbis

⭐ American Girl®

Name: American Quarter Horse
Color: Any solid
Characteristics:
Can run a quarter mile faster
than any other breed

© iStockphoto/kycstudio

⭐ American Girl®

Name: American Belgian
Color: Mostly red roan, chestnut,
and sorrel (light chestnut)
Characteristics:
Draft horse; weighs just over a ton;
very muscular and able to pull an
amazing amount of weight

© Grant Heilman/Grant Heilman
Photography, Inc.

⭐ American Girl®

Name: Shire
Color: Bay, black, brown, or gray
Characteristics:
Draft horse; pulls up to five tons; legs
often have white stockings with long
hairs or "feathers"

© iStockphoto/aquasolid

⭐ American Girl®

Name: Friesian
Color: Solid black
Characteristics:
Beautiful rare breed;
high-stepping and athletic

© iStockphoto/kerrick

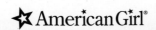

Name: Andalusian
Color: Gray, bay, or white
Characteristics:
Spirited and athletic

© Juniors Bildarchiv

Name: Arabian
Color: Chestnut, bay, or black
Characteristics:
Small head and a dished (concave) face; elegant, graceful, loyal, friendly, and curious

© Gemma Giannini/Grant Heilman Photography, Inc.

☆ AmericanGirl®

Name: Miniature Horse
Color: Any
Characteristics:
Tiny version of a regular horse; kept primarily as a pet

© Gemma Giannini/Grant Heilman Photography, Inc.

☆ AmericanGirl®

Name: Connemara Pony
Color: Usually gray; also bay, black, brown, or dun
Characteristics:
Excellent jumper suitable for adults and children

© Michael St. Maur Sheil/Corbis

☆ AmericanGirl®

Name: Thoroughbred
Color: Most solids
Characteristics:
Fastest horse in the world; spunky and temperamental

© Gemma Giannini/Grant Heilman Photography, Inc.

☆ AmericanGirl®

Name: Clydesdale
Color: Bay, brown, or black, with white markings around the face and feet
Characteristics:
Eager-to-work draft horse with thickly "feathered" feet; has a consistently gentle nature

© Kelly-Mooney Photography/Corbis

 ☆ AmericanGirl®

Name: Shetland Pony
Color: Any
Characteristics:
Small-sized pony; popular horse for children; gentle and very smart

© Kevin Schafer/Corbis

☆ AmericanGirl®

Name: Percheron
Color: Gray or black
Characteristics:
Draft horse; weighs more
than a ton; calm nature

© Linda Dufurrena/Grant Heilman Photography

Name: Appaloosa
Color: Spots unique to each horse.
Basic patterns include blanket,
marble, leopard, snowflake, and frost.
Characteristics:
Quiet, willing, and gentle

© iStockphoto/jeanma85

Name: Tennessee Walking Horse
Color: Any solid
Characteristics:
Unique running walk with high-
stepping front feet; straight head
with large ears; easygoing

© iStockphoto/dcdebs

Name: American Paint Horse
Color: Broad pinto spotting: mostly
white with dark patches, such as
black, brown, or chestnut—or
mostly dark with white patches
Characteristics:
Mellow, easygoing, and smart

© iStockphoto/John Pitcher

Name: Morgan
Color: Bay, brown, chestnut, or black
Characteristics:
Small head, arched neck,
and short legs; strong, gentle,
and eager to please

© Kit Houghton
Photography/Corbis

Name: Mustang
Color: Any
Characteristics:
Hardy and intelligent; descendant of
the first horses brought to America
by the Spanish in the 1500s

© iStockphoto/ivanastar

Yee-ha-ha!

More filly funnies for a few horselaughs!

What do you get when you cross a horse with the person who lives in the house next door?

a neigh-bor

What did one horse say when she met another horse?

"The pace is familiar, but I can't recall your mane."

Why can't horses dance?

Because they have two left feet

What sickness is the most common with horses?

hay fever

What dressing do horses put on their salads?

ranch

Why do horse fans like to get to bed early?

They can't wait to see their night mares.

Pretty Ponies

Ride around town with one of these perfect ponytails.

Flip Tail

Flip for a new twist on the classic ponytail.

1. Hold your chin down toward your chest and make a low ponytail. Tie it off with an elastic.

2. Reach underneath the ponytail and use your finger and thumb to make a hole in the middle of your hair above the elastic.

3. With your other hand, twist the ponytail, grab it with your fingers that are making the hole, and pull it through.

Ponytail Wrap

Use a strand of hair to band a ponytail.

1. Hold your chin down toward your chest and make a low ponytail, leaving a 1-inch strand of hair underneath the tail out of the elastic.

2. Wrap the loose strand around the elastic 2 or 3 times.

3. Tuck the rest of the strand into the elastic under the ponytail, and pull through. Comb the strand into the tail.

Along the Line

Find the differences between this picture and the poster at right.

Good friends stick together!

You'll find the answers in the back of the book.

Writing Lessons

For clever crafts, cards, and correspondence, doodle riding gear on a hand-drawn alphabet.

Pony Points

The basic parts of a horse or pony are called its "points." Study these basic points, and then see if you can identify them on a different horse picture.

Book Branding

Personalize your books with these equine bookplates.

Property of
Circle Ranch

Owner:

Straight from the
horse's mouth,
this book belongs
to

Gallop . . .

canter . . .

trot . . . walk . . .

whoa!

This book is the property of

Hold your horses!

This book
belongs to me.

Horse Gear

Trot around school with horse-inspired supplies.

Cowgirl Cover

Cut a strip off a bandanna, and fold the sides into the center. Wrap the folded bandanna around a journal cover, taping the ends to the inside cover. Attach a horse appliqué with craft glue. Let dry.

Bronco Bookmark

Slide a horse shank button (the kind with the loop on the back) onto a fancy bobby pin. Slip the bobby pin onto the page to mark your spot

Tack Room

Cover your world with sweet horse stickers.

Use these stickers to create art for your room.
- Press them onto a binder.
- Decorate stationery, a folder, or a bulletin board.
- Accent a frame.
- Attach them to a jar for a pencil cup.
- Press the stickers into a pleasing pattern on the back of a hairbrush. Cover with a few coats of Mod Podge, if you like. Let dry completely.

Ask an adult for permission before you permanently attach any stickers.

U ★ RIDE 'EM!   I ♥ Horses

Pony Pride

Congratulations! You're now a horse-project professional.
Display this poster in honor of your accomplishment.

Answers: Along the Line

If horses aren't your only passion, let us know. Tell us about your other interests at the address below.

Write to:

"Oodles of" Editor
American Girl
8400 Fairway Place
Middleton, WI 53562

All comments and suggestions received by American Girl may be used without compensation or acknowledgment. Sorry, photos can't be returned.

Here are some other American Girl books you might like:

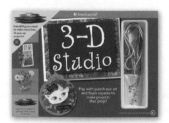

☐ I read it.

☐ I read it.

☐ I read it.

☐ I read it.

☐ I read it.

☐ I read it.

☐ I read it.

☐ I read it.